100 Day

Gong

& Gratitude Journal

This journal belongs to: _____

ISBN-13: 978-1-7268-0104-1

DEDICATION

This journal is dedicated to everyone who strives to live fully and help others do the same.

What is a Gong?

Gong is a Chinese term referring to a "skill cultivated through steady practice." The 100 Day Gong draws on this ancient Chinese Taoist tradition of "cultivation practice." To complete a gong, simply commit to performing a certain action that will improve your wellness for 100 days in a row. If you miss a day, start over at day one. This journal includes enough calendars for three gongs and plenty of journal pages to last six months.

Why 100 Days?

To live in wellness, it is important to create health-promoting habits that become automatic and no longer require our precious and limited will-power. While very simple habits can be formed in 21 days or even less, meaningful habits take much longer to establish. After 100 days of effort, you will find that the healthy benefits you experience will continue with ease for many years to come.

How do I use this journal?

Begin. Do not delay your progress until you think you have the "perfect" gong and timing. Ask yourself right now, "What is the one thing I wish I had time to do that would help me feel good?" Select an "easy" version of this goal as your gong. If you want to run five miles every day, commit to running one. If you want to write a book, commit to writing five minutes every day. Use the Gong Calendar to mark your progress by crossing out the box each day. In your journal, reflect on the last 24 hours and write three new things you are grateful for and why. The smaller and more specific these things are, the better. Use the journal space to write about the most meaningful experience you had in the previous day.

When you use this journal to set your wellness intention and record your joys along the way, you will be tapping in to the vast power of your subconscious mind to cultivate your happiest and healthiest self. The effects are lasting and powerful. Enjoy!

Acknowledgement and Resources

I want to thank Pedram Shojai, OMD, a former Taoist monk and now physician of Chinese medicine, for introducing me to the idea of a 100 Day Gong. I first learned about this powerful technique for developing personal discipline from his 2014 podcast episode of The Health Bridge with Dr. Sara Gottfried. I have completed at least one 100 Day Gong every year since then, and my health and happiness continue to thrive as a result of this practice.

To learn more about the incredible work Dr. Shojai is doing to improve the health of individuals and our world, visit **theurbanmonk.com** and **well.org**.

I also want to thank Shawn Achor, happiness researcher, author, and inspiring speaker, for the work he is doing to bridge the gap between academic research in positive psychology and the real world where these findings are so urgently needed. He shared the evidence-based gratitude and journaling practices utilized in this journal in a Calm Meditation App Masterclass on happiness as well as his book, "Big Potential."

Visit his website **goodthinkinc.com** and read his fun and informative books to learn more about the science demonstrating how happiness leads to success, not the other way around.

Thank you to my husband and best friend, Cullen, for doing your own gong, and for all you do to help our family be happy and healthy.

"Health is a matter of choice,
not a mystery of chance."

— Aristotle

GONG: Fitness Journey

			1			
2	3	4	5	6	7	8
9	10	11	12	13	14	15
16	17	18	19	20	21	22
23	24	25	26	27	28	29
30	31	32	33	34	35	36
37	38	39	40	41	42	43
44	45	46	47	48	49	50
51	52	53	54	55	56	57
58	59	60	61	62	63	64
65	66	67	68	69	70	71
72	73	74	75	76	77	78
79	80	81	82	83	84	85
86	87	88	89	90	91	92
93	94	95	96	97	98	99
			100			

"Knowing others is intelligence;
knowing yourself is true wisdom.
Mastering others is strength;
mastering yourself is true power."
— Lao Tzu, Tao Te Ching

GONG: _____

			1			
2	3	4	5	6	7	8
9	10	11	12	13	14	15
16	17	18	19	20	21	22
23	24	25	26	27	28	29
30	31	32	33	34	35	36
37	38	39	40	41	42	43
44	45	46	47	48	49	50
51	52	53	54	55	56	57
58	59	60	61	62	63	64
65	66	67	68	69	70	71
72	73	74	75	76	77	78
79	80	81	82	83	84	85
86	87	88	89	90	91	92
93	94	95	96	97	98	99
			100			

"Happiness is not the belief that we don't need to change; it's the realization that we can."

— Shawn Achor

GONG: _____

			1			
2	3	4	5	6	7	8
9	10	11	12	13	14	15
16	17	18	19	20	21	22
23	24	25	26	27	28	29
30	31	32	33	34	35	36
37	38	39	40	41	42	43
44	45	46	47	48	49	50
51	52	53	54	55	56	57
58	59	60	61	62	63	64
65	66	67	68	69	70	71
72	73	74	75	76	77	78
79	80	81	82	83	84	85
86	87	88	89	90	91	92
93	94	95	96	97	98	99
			100			

"Do not be concerned with the fruit of your action-just give attention to the action itself. The fruit will come of its own accord."

— Eckhart Tolle

☐ Gong Day #_____ M T W R F S S _____/_____/20_____

Today I am Grateful:

- _____

because_____

- _____

because_____

- _____

because_____

Most meaningful Experience Journal:

_____
_____
_____
_____
_____
_____
_____
_____
_____
_____
_____
_____
_____
_____
_____
_____
_____
_____
_____
_____
_____

☐ *Gong* Day #_____   M T W R F S S   ____ / ____ / 20 ____

Today **I am** Grateful:

- _____

because_____

- _____

because_____

- _____

because_____

Most meaningful **Experience** Journal:

_____
_____
_____
_____
_____
_____
_____
_____
_____
_____
_____
_____
_____
_____
_____
_____
_____
_____

□ *Gong* Day #_____ M T W R F S S ____ / ____ / 20 ____

Today **I am** Grateful:

- _____

  because_____

- _____

  because_____

- _____

  because_____

Most meaningful **Experience** Journal:

_____
_____
_____
_____
_____
_____
_____
_____
_____
_____
_____
_____
_____
_____
_____
_____
_____
_____
_____

□ Gong Day #_____   M T W R F S S   ____/ ____/ 20 _____

Today I am Grateful:

- _____

because_____

- _____

because_____

- _____

because_____

Most meaningful Experience Journal:

_____
_____
_____
_____
_____
_____
_____
_____
_____
_____
_____
_____
_____
_____
_____
_____
_____
_____

□ *Gong* Day #_____   M T W R F S S   _____ / _____ / 20 _____

Today **I am** Grateful:

- _____

  because_____

- _____

  because_____

- _____

  because_____

Most meaningful **Experience** Journal:

_____
_____
_____
_____
_____
_____
_____
_____
_____
_____
_____
_____
_____
_____
_____
_____
_____
_____
_____

☐ Gong Day #_____ M T W R F S S _____ / _____ / 20 _____

Today **I am** Grateful:

- _____

  because_____

- _____

  because_____

- _____

  because_____

Most meaningful **Experience** Journal:

_____
_____
_____
_____
_____
_____
_____
_____
_____
_____
_____
_____
_____
_____
_____
_____
_____
_____
_____

□ Gong Day #_____   M T W R F S S   _____ / _____ / 20 _____

Today I am Grateful:

- _____

  because_____

- _____

  because_____

- _____

  because_____

Most meaningful Experience Journal:

_____
_____
_____
_____
_____
_____
_____
_____
_____
_____
_____
_____
_____
_____
_____
_____
_____
_____
_____
_____

□ Gong Day #_____   M T W R F S S   ____ / ____ / 20 ____

Today I am Grateful:

- _____

because_____

- _____

because_____

- _____

because_____

Most meaningful Experience Journal:

_____
_____
_____
_____
_____
_____
_____
_____
_____
_____
_____
_____
_____
_____
_____
_____
_____
_____
_____

☐ Gong Day #_____   M T W R F S S   ____ / ____ / 20 ____

Today I am Grateful:

■ _____

because_____

■ _____

because_____

■ _____

because_____

Most meaningful Experience Journal:

_____
_____
_____
_____
_____
_____
_____
_____
_____
_____
_____
_____
_____
_____
_____
_____
_____
_____
_____

□ Gong Day #_____   M T W R F S S   ____/____/20____

Today I am Grateful:

- _____

  because_____

- _____

  because_____

- _____

  because_____

Most meaningful Experience Journal:

_____
_____
_____
_____
_____
_____
_____
_____
_____
_____
_____
_____
_____
_____
_____
_____
_____
_____

☐ *Gong* Day #_____ M T W R F S S _____ / _____ / 20 _____

Today I am Grateful:

- _____

  because_____

- _____

  because_____

- _____

  because_____

Most meaningful Experience Journal:

_____

_____

_____

_____

_____

_____

_____

_____

_____

_____

_____

_____

_____

_____

_____

_____

_____

_____

□ Gong Day #_____   M T W R F S S   ____/____/20____

Today I am Grateful:

■ _____

because_____

■ _____

because_____

■ _____

because_____

Most meaningful Experience Journal:

_____
_____
_____
_____
_____
_____
_____
_____
_____
_____
_____
_____
_____
_____
_____
_____
_____
_____
_____
_____
_____

□ *Gong* Day #_____   M T W R F S S   ____ / ____ / 20 ____

Today I am Grateful:

- _____

because_____

- _____

because_____

- _____

because_____

Most meaningful Experience Journal:

_____
_____
_____
_____
_____
_____
_____
_____
_____
_____
_____
_____
_____
_____
_____
_____
_____
_____

☐ *Gong* Day #_____   M T W R F S S   ____ / ____ / 20 ____

Today **I am** Grateful:

- _____

because_____

- _____

because_____

- _____

because_____

Most meaningful **Experience** Journal:

_____
_____
_____
_____
_____
_____
_____
_____
_____
_____
_____
_____
_____
_____
_____
_____
_____
_____
_____

□ Gong Day #_____ M T W R F S S ____/____/20____

Today I am Grateful:

- _____

  because_____

- _____

  because_____

- _____

  because_____

Most meaningful Experience Journal:

_____
_____
_____
_____
_____
_____
_____
_____
_____
_____
_____
_____
_____
_____
_____
_____
_____
_____
_____

☐ Gong Day #_____ M T W R F S S ____/____/20____

Today **I am** Grateful:

- _____

  because_____

- _____

  because_____

- _____

  because_____

Most meaningful **Experience** Journal:

_____
_____
_____
_____
_____
_____
_____
_____
_____
_____
_____
_____
_____
_____
_____
_____
_____
_____
_____
_____

□ *Gong* Day #_____   M T W R F S S   ____ / ____ / 20 _____

Today **I am** Grateful:

- _____

because_____

- _____

because_____

- _____

because_____

Most meaningful **Experience** Journal:

_____
_____
_____
_____
_____
_____
_____
_____
_____
_____
_____
_____
_____
_____
_____
_____
_____
_____
_____
_____
_____

☐ *Gong* Day #_____ M T W R F S S ____/ ____/ 20 ____

Today **I am** Grateful:

- _____

  because_____

- _____

  because_____

- _____

  because_____

Most meaningful **Experience** Journal:

□ Gong Day #_____ M T W R F S S ____ / ____ / 20 ____

Today I am Grateful:

- _____

  because_____

- _____

  because_____

- _____

  because_____

Most meaningful Experience Journal:

_____
_____
_____
_____
_____
_____
_____
_____
_____
_____
_____
_____
_____
_____
_____
_____
_____
_____
_____

□ *Gong* Day #_____   M T W R F S S   ____ / ____ / 20 ____

Today **I am** Grateful:

- _____

  because_____

- _____

  because_____

- _____

  because_____

Most meaningful **Experience** Journal:

_____
_____
_____
_____
_____
_____
_____
_____
_____
_____
_____
_____
_____
_____
_____
_____
_____
_____
_____

☐ *Gong* Day #_____   M   T   W   R   F   S   S   ____ / ____ / 20 _____

Today **I am** Grateful:

- _____

  because_____

- _____

  because_____

- _____

  because_____

Most meaningful **Experience** Journal:

_____
_____
_____
_____
_____
_____
_____
_____
_____
_____
_____
_____
_____
_____
_____
_____
_____
_____
_____
_____

☐ Gong Day #_____ M T W R F S S ____ / ____ / 20 ____

Today I am Grateful:

- _____

because_____

- _____

because_____

- _____

because_____

Most meaningful Experience Journal:

_____
_____
_____
_____
_____
_____
_____
_____
_____
_____
_____
_____
_____
_____
_____
_____
_____
_____
_____

□ Gong Day #_____   M T W R F S S   ____ / ____ / 20 ____

Today I am Grateful:

- _____

  because_____

- _____

  because_____

- _____

  because_____

Most meaningful Experience Journal:

_____
_____
_____
_____
_____
_____
_____
_____
_____
_____
_____
_____
_____
_____
_____
_____
_____
_____
_____
_____

☐ Gong Day #_____ M T W R F S S _____ / _____ / 20 _____

Today I am Grateful:

- _____

  because_____

- _____

  because_____

- _____

  because_____

Most meaningful Experience Journal:

_____
_____
_____
_____
_____
_____
_____
_____
_____
_____
_____
_____
_____
_____
_____
_____
_____
_____
_____

□ Gong Day #_____   M T W R F S S   ____/ ____/ 20 ____

Today I am Grateful:

- _____

because_____

- _____

because_____

- _____

because_____

Most meaningful Experience Journal:

_____
_____
_____
_____
_____
_____
_____
_____
_____
_____
_____
_____
_____
_____
_____
_____
_____
_____
_____

□ *Gong* Day #_____ M T W R F S S ____ / ____ / 20 ____

Today **I am** Grateful:

- _____

because_____

- _____

because_____

- _____

because_____

Most meaningful **Experience** Journal:

_____
_____
_____
_____
_____
_____
_____
_____
_____
_____
_____
_____
_____
_____
_____
_____
_____
_____
_____

□ Gong Day #_____ M T W R F S S ____/____/20____

Today I am Grateful:

- _____

  because_____

- _____

  because_____

- _____

  because_____

Most meaningful Experience Journal:

_____
_____
_____
_____
_____
_____
_____
_____
_____
_____
_____
_____
_____
_____
_____
_____
_____
_____
_____
_____

☐ Gong Day #_____   M T W R F S S   ____ / ____ / 20 ____

Today I am Grateful:

- _____

  because_____

- _____

  because_____

- _____

  because_____

Most meaningful Experience Journal:

_____
_____
_____
_____
_____
_____
_____
_____
_____
_____
_____
_____
_____
_____
_____
_____
_____
_____
_____

□ *Gong* Day #_____   M T W R F S S   ____ / ____ / 20 ____

Today I **am** Grateful:

- _____

  because_____

- _____

  because_____

- _____

  because_____

Most meaningful **Experience** Journal:

_____
_____
_____
_____
_____
_____
_____
_____
_____
_____
_____
_____
_____
_____
_____
_____
_____
_____
_____
_____
_____

□ Gong Day #_____   M T W R F S S   ____ / ____ / 20 ____

Today I am Grateful:

- _____

  because_____

- _____

  because_____

- _____

  because_____

Most meaningful Experience Journal:

_____
_____
_____
_____
_____
_____
_____
_____
_____
_____
_____
_____
_____
_____
_____
_____
_____
_____
_____

□ Gong Day #_____   M T W R F S S   ____ / ____ / 20 ____

Today I am Grateful:

- _____

  because_____

- _____

  because_____

- _____

  because_____

Most meaningful Experience Journal:

_____
_____
_____
_____
_____
_____
_____
_____
_____
_____
_____
_____
_____
_____
_____
_____
_____
_____
_____

□ Gong Day #_____   M T W R F S S   _____ / _____ / 20 _____

Today I am Grateful:

- _____

because_____

- _____

because_____

- _____

because_____

Most meaningful Experience Journal:

_____
_____
_____
_____
_____
_____
_____
_____
_____
_____
_____
_____
_____
_____
_____
_____
_____
_____

□ Gong Day #_____   M T W R F S S   ____/____/20____

Today I am Grateful:

- _____

  because_____

- _____

  because_____

- _____

  because_____

Most meaningful Experience Journal:

_____
_____
_____
_____
_____
_____
_____
_____
_____
_____
_____
_____
_____
_____
_____
_____
_____
_____
_____

□ Gong Day #_____   M T W R F S S   ____/____/20____

Today I am Grateful:

- _____

  because_____

- _____

  because_____

- _____

  because_____

Most meaningful Experience Journal:

_____
_____
_____
_____
_____
_____
_____
_____
_____
_____
_____
_____
_____
_____
_____
_____
_____
_____

□ Gong Day #_____   M T W R F S S   ____/____/20____

Today I am Grateful:

- _____

because_____

- _____

because_____

- _____

because_____

Most meaningful Experience Journal:

_____
_____
_____
_____
_____
_____
_____
_____
_____
_____
_____
_____
_____
_____
_____
_____
_____
_____
_____
_____

□ Gong Day #_____   M T W R F S S   ____/____/20____

Today **I am** Grateful:

- _____

because_____

- _____

because_____

- _____

because_____

Most meaningful **Experience** Journal:

_____
_____
_____
_____
_____
_____
_____
_____
_____
_____
_____
_____
_____
_____
_____
_____
_____
_____
_____

□ *Gong* Day #_____   M T W R F S S   ____ / ____ / 20 ____

Today **I am** Grateful:

- _____

  because_____

- _____

  because_____

- _____

  because_____

Most meaningful **Experience** Journal:

_____
_____
_____
_____
_____
_____
_____
_____
_____
_____
_____
_____
_____
_____
_____
_____
_____
_____
_____

□ Gong Day #_____   M T W R F S S   _____ / _____ / 20 _____

Today I am Grateful:

- _____

because_____

- _____

because_____

- _____

because_____

Most meaningful Experience Journal:

_____
_____
_____
_____
_____
_____
_____
_____
_____
_____
_____
_____
_____
_____
_____
_____
_____
_____
_____

□ *Gong* Day #_____   M T W R F S S   ____ / ____ / 20 ____

Today **I am** Grateful:

- _____

  because_____

- _____

  because_____

- _____

  because_____

Most meaningful **Experience** Journal:

_____
_____
_____
_____
_____
_____
_____
_____
_____
_____
_____
_____
_____
_____
_____
_____
_____
_____
_____

□ Gong Day #_____   M T W R F S S   ____ / ____ / 20 ____

Today **I am** Grateful:

- _____

  because_____

- _____

  because_____

- _____

  because_____

Most meaningful **Experience** Journal:

_____
_____
_____
_____
_____
_____
_____
_____
_____
_____
_____
_____
_____
_____
_____
_____
_____
_____
_____

□ *Gong* Day #_____   M T W R F S S   ____ / ____ / 20 ____

Today I am Grateful:

- _____

   because_____

- _____

   because_____

- _____

   because_____

Most meaningful Experience Journal:

_____
_____
_____
_____
_____
_____
_____
_____
_____
_____
_____
_____
_____
_____
_____
_____
_____
_____
_____

□ Gong Day #_____   M T W R F S S   ____ / ____ / 20 ____

Today **I am** Grateful:

■ _____

because_____

■ _____

because_____

■ _____

because_____

Most meaningful **Experience** Journal:

_____
_____
_____
_____
_____
_____
_____
_____
_____
_____
_____
_____
_____
_____
_____
_____
_____
_____
_____
_____

□ Gong Day #_____ M T W R F S S ____ / ____ / 20 ____

Today I am Grateful:

- _____

  because_____

- _____

  because_____

- _____

  because_____

Most meaningful Experience Journal:

_____
_____
_____
_____
_____
_____
_____
_____
_____
_____
_____
_____
_____
_____
_____
_____
_____
_____
_____
_____

□ Gong Day #_____   M T W R F S S   ____ / ____ / 20 ____

Today I am Grateful:

- _____

because_____

- _____

because_____

- _____

because_____

Most meaningful Experience Journal:

_____
_____
_____
_____
_____
_____
_____
_____
_____
_____
_____
_____
_____
_____
_____
_____
_____
_____
_____

□ Gong Day #_____   M T W R F S S   ____ / ____ / 20 ____

Today I am Grateful:

■ _____

because_____

■ _____

because_____

■ _____

because_____

Most meaningful Experience Journal:

_____
_____
_____
_____
_____
_____
_____
_____
_____
_____
_____
_____
_____
_____
_____
_____
_____
_____
_____
_____

□ Gong Day #_____ M T W R F S S ____ / ____ / 20 ____

Today I am Grateful:

- _____

because_____

- _____

because_____

- _____

because_____

Most meaningful Experience Journal:

_____
_____
_____
_____
_____
_____
_____
_____
_____
_____
_____
_____
_____
_____
_____
_____
_____
_____

□ Gong Day #_____   M T W R F S S   ____/ ____/ 20 ____

Today I am Grateful:

- _____

  because_____

- _____

  because_____

- _____

  because_____

Most meaningful Experience Journal:

_____
_____
_____
_____
_____
_____
_____
_____
_____
_____
_____
_____
_____
_____
_____
_____
_____
_____
_____

□ Gong Day #_____   M T W R F S S   ____ / ____ / 20 ____

Today I am Grateful:

- _____

  because_____

- _____

  because_____

- _____

  because_____

Most meaningful Experience Journal:

_____
_____
_____
_____
_____
_____
_____
_____
_____
_____
_____
_____
_____
_____
_____
_____
_____
_____

□ *Gong* Day #_____   M T W R F S S   ____/____/ 20____

Today **I am** Grateful:

- _____

because_____

- _____

because_____

- _____

because_____

Most meaningful **Experience** Journal:

_____
_____
_____
_____
_____
_____
_____
_____
_____
_____
_____
_____
_____
_____
_____
_____
_____
_____

☐ *Gong* Day #_____ M T W R F S S _____ / _____ / 20 _____

Today **I am** Grateful:

- _____

because_____

- _____

because_____

- _____

because_____

Most meaningful **Experience** Journal:

_____

_____

_____

_____

_____

_____

_____

_____

_____

_____

_____

_____

_____

_____

_____

_____

_____

_____

□ *Gong* Day #_____ M T W R F S S ____ / ____ / 20 ____

Today I *am* Grateful:

■ _____

because_____

■ _____

because_____

■ _____

because_____

Most meaningful **Experience** Journal:

_____
_____
_____
_____
_____
_____
_____
_____
_____
_____
_____
_____
_____
_____
_____
_____
_____
_____

☐ Gong Day #_____ M T W R F S S ____ / ____ / 20 ____

Today I am Grateful:

- _____

because_____

- _____

because_____

- _____

because_____

Most meaningful Experience Journal:

_____
_____
_____
_____
_____
_____
_____
_____
_____
_____
_____
_____
_____
_____
_____
_____
_____
_____

□ *Gong* Day #_____   M T W R F S S   ____ / ____ / 20 ____

Today **I am** Grateful:

- _____

because_____

- _____

because_____

- _____

because_____

Most meaningful **Experience** Journal:

_____
_____
_____
_____
_____
_____
_____
_____
_____
_____
_____
_____
_____
_____
_____
_____
_____
_____
_____

□ Gong Day #_____   M T W R F S S   ____ / ____ / 20 ____

Today **I am** Grateful:

- _____

  because_____

- _____

  because_____

- _____

  because_____

Most meaningful **Experience** Journal:

_____
_____
_____
_____
_____
_____
_____
_____
_____
_____
_____
_____
_____
_____
_____
_____
_____
_____
_____

□ *Gong* Day #_____   M T W R F S S   ____/____/20____

Today **I am** Grateful:

- _____

  because_____

- _____

  because_____

- _____

  because_____

Most meaningful **Experience** Journal:

_____

_____

_____

_____

_____

_____

_____

_____

_____

_____

_____

_____

_____

_____

_____

_____

_____

_____

_____

□ Gong Day #_____   M T W R F S S   ____ / ____ / 20 ____

Today I am Grateful:

- _____

  because_____

- _____

  because_____

- _____

  because_____

Most meaningful Experience Journal:

_____
_____
_____
_____
_____
_____
_____
_____
_____
_____
_____
_____
_____
_____
_____
_____
_____
_____

□ Gong Day #_____   M T W R F S S   ____ / ____ / 20 ____

Today I am Grateful:

- _____

  because_____

- _____

  because_____

- _____

  because_____

Most meaningful Experience Journal:

_____
_____
_____
_____
_____
_____
_____
_____
_____
_____
_____
_____
_____
_____
_____
_____
_____
_____

□ Gong Day #_____   M T W R F S S   _____ / _____ / 20 _____

Today I am Grateful:

■ _____

because_____

■ _____

because_____

■ _____

because_____

Most meaningful Experience Journal:

_____
_____
_____
_____
_____
_____
_____
_____
_____
_____
_____
_____
_____
_____
_____
_____
_____
_____

□ Gong Day #_____   M T W R F S S   ____/ ____/ 20 ____

Today I am Grateful:

- _____

  because_____

- _____

  because_____

- _____

  because_____

Most meaningful Experience Journal:

_____
_____
_____
_____
_____
_____
_____
_____
_____
_____
_____
_____
_____
_____
_____
_____
_____
_____
_____

☐ Gong Day #_____ M T W R F S S ____ / ____ / 20 ____

Today I am Grateful:

- _____

  because_____

- _____

  because_____

- _____

  because_____

Most meaningful Experience Journal:

_____
_____
_____
_____
_____
_____
_____
_____
_____
_____
_____
_____
_____
_____
_____
_____
_____
_____

□ *Gong* Day #_____   M T W R F S S   ____ / ____ / 20 ____

Today **I am** Grateful:

- _____

  because_____

- _____

  because_____

- _____

  because_____

Most meaningful **Experience** Journal:

_____
_____
_____
_____
_____
_____
_____
_____
_____
_____
_____
_____
_____
_____
_____
_____
_____
_____

□ Gong Day #_____   M T W R F S S   ____ / ____ / 20 ____

Today **I am** Grateful:

- _____

because_____

- _____

because_____

- _____

because_____

Most meaningful **Experience** Journal:

_____
_____
_____
_____
_____
_____
_____
_____
_____
_____
_____
_____
_____
_____
_____
_____
_____

□ Gong Day #_____   M T W R F S S   ____/____/20____

Today I am Grateful:

- _____

  because_____

- _____

  because_____

- _____

  because_____

Most meaningful Experience Journal:

_____
_____
_____
_____
_____
_____
_____
_____
_____
_____
_____
_____
_____
_____
_____
_____
_____
_____
_____

☐ Gong Day #_____   M T W R F S S   ____ / ____ / 20 ____

Today **I am** Grateful:

- _____

because_____

- _____

because_____

- _____

because_____

Most meaningful **Experience** Journal:

_____
_____
_____
_____
_____
_____
_____
_____
_____
_____
_____
_____
_____
_____
_____
_____
_____
_____
_____

□ *Gong* Day #_____ M T W R F S S _____ / _____ / 20 _____

Today **I am** Grateful:

■ _____

because_____

■ _____

because_____

■ _____

because_____

Most meaningful **Experience** Journal:

_____
_____
_____
_____
_____
_____
_____
_____
_____
_____
_____
_____
_____
_____
_____
_____
_____
_____
_____
_____

☐ Gong Day #_____ M T W R F S S ____ / ____ / 20 ____

Today **I am** Grateful:

- _____

  because_____

- _____

  because_____

- _____

  because_____

Most meaningful **Experience** Journal:

_____
_____
_____
_____
_____
_____
_____
_____
_____
_____
_____
_____
_____
_____
_____
_____
_____
_____

□ *Gong* Day #_____   M T W R F S S   _____ / _____ / 20 _____

Today **I am** Grateful:

- _____

  because_____

- _____

  because_____

- _____

  because_____

Most meaningful **Experience** Journal:

_____
_____
_____
_____
_____
_____
_____
_____
_____
_____
_____
_____
_____
_____
_____
_____
_____
_____
_____

☐ Gong Day #_____   M T W R F S S   ____ / ____ / 20 ____

Today I am Grateful:

- _____

because_____

- _____

because_____

- _____

because_____

Most meaningful Experience Journal:

_____
_____
_____
_____
_____
_____
_____
_____
_____
_____
_____
_____
_____
_____
_____
_____
_____
_____

□ Gong Day #_____   M T W R F S S   ____ / ____ / 20 ____

Today I am Grateful:

■ _____

because_____

■ _____

because_____

■ _____

because_____

Most meaningful Experience Journal:

_____
_____
_____
_____
_____
_____
_____
_____
_____
_____
_____
_____
_____
_____
_____
_____
_____
_____
_____
_____

□ Gong Day #_____   M T W R F S S   ____ / ____ / 20 ____

Today I am Grateful:

- _____

  because_____

- _____

  because_____

- _____

  because_____

Most meaningful Experience Journal:

_____
_____
_____
_____
_____
_____
_____
_____
_____
_____
_____
_____
_____
_____
_____
_____
_____
_____
_____

□ Gong Day #_____   M T W R F S S   ____/____/20____

Today I am Grateful:

- _____

  because_____

- _____

  because_____

- _____

  because_____

Most meaningful Experience Journal:

_____
_____
_____
_____
_____
_____
_____
_____
_____
_____
_____
_____
_____
_____
_____
_____
_____
_____
_____

☐ Gong Day #_____   M T W R F S S   ____ / ____ / 20 ____

Today **I am** Grateful:

- _____

  because_____

- _____

  because_____

- _____

  because_____

Most meaningful **Experience** Journal:

_____
_____
_____
_____
_____
_____
_____
_____
_____
_____
_____
_____
_____
_____
_____
_____
_____
_____
_____
_____

□ *Gong* Day #_____   M T W R F S S   _____ / _____ / 20 _____

Today **I am** Grateful:

- _____

because_____

- _____

because_____

- _____

because_____

Most meaningful **Experience** Journal:

_____
_____
_____
_____
_____
_____
_____
_____
_____
_____
_____
_____
_____
_____
_____
_____
_____
_____
_____

☐ Gong Day #_____ M T W R F S S _____ / _____ / 20 _____

Today I am Grateful:

- _____

because_____

- _____

because_____

- _____

because_____

Most meaningful Experience Journal:

_____
_____
_____
_____
_____
_____
_____
_____
_____
_____
_____
_____
_____
_____
_____
_____
_____
_____

□ *Gong* Day #_____   M T W R F S S   ____ / ____ / 20 _____

Today **I am** Grateful:

- _____

because_____

- _____

because_____

- _____

because_____

Most meaningful **Experience** Journal:

_____
_____
_____
_____
_____
_____
_____
_____
_____
_____
_____
_____
_____
_____
_____
_____
_____
_____
_____

□ Gong Day #_____   M T W R F S S   ____ / ____ / 20 ____

Today **I am** Grateful:

- _____

  because_____

- _____

  because_____

- _____

  because_____

Most meaningful **Experience** Journal:

_____

_____

_____

_____

_____

_____

_____

_____

_____

_____

_____

_____

_____

_____

_____

_____

_____

_____

_____

□ Gong Day #_____ M T W R F S S _____ / _____ / 20 _____

Today I am Grateful:

- _____

  because_____

- _____

  because_____

- _____

  because_____

Most meaningful Experience Journal:

_____
_____
_____
_____
_____
_____
_____
_____
_____
_____
_____
_____
_____
_____
_____
_____
_____
_____
_____

□ Gong Day #_____   M T W R F S S   ____ / ____ / 20 _____

Today **I am** Grateful:

- _____

because_____

- _____

because_____

- _____

because_____

Most meaningful **Experience** Journal:

_____
_____
_____
_____
_____
_____
_____
_____
_____
_____
_____
_____
_____
_____
_____
_____
_____
_____
_____

□ Gong Day #_____   M T W R F S S   ____ / ____ / 20 ____

Today I am Grateful:

■ _____

because_____

■ _____

because_____

■ _____

because_____

Most meaningful Experience Journal:

_____
_____
_____
_____
_____
_____
_____
_____
_____
_____
_____
_____
_____
_____
_____
_____
_____
_____
_____
_____

☐ *Gong* Day #_____   M T W R F S S   _____ / _____ / 20 _____

Today **I am** Grateful:

- _____

because_____

- _____

because_____

- _____

because_____

Most meaningful **Experience** Journal:

_____
_____
_____
_____
_____
_____
_____
_____
_____
_____
_____
_____
_____
_____
_____
_____
_____
_____
_____

☐ Gong Day #_____   M T W R F S S   ____ / ____ / 20 ____

Today I am Grateful:

■ _____

because_____

■ _____

because_____

■ _____

because_____

Most meaningful Experience Journal:

_____

_____

_____

_____

_____

_____

_____

_____

_____

_____

_____

_____

_____

_____

_____

_____

_____

_____

□ Gong Day #_____   M T W R F S S   ____ / ____ / 20 ____

Today I am Grateful:

- _____

because_____

- _____

because_____

- _____

because_____

Most meaningful Experience Journal:

_____
_____
_____
_____
_____
_____
_____
_____
_____
_____
_____
_____
_____
_____
_____
_____
_____
_____
_____

□ Gong Day #_____ M T W R F S S ____/____/20____

Today I am Grateful:

- _____

  because_____

- _____

  because_____

- _____

  because_____

Most meaningful Experience Journal:

_____
_____
_____
_____
_____
_____
_____
_____
_____
_____
_____
_____
_____
_____
_____
_____
_____
_____
_____

☐ Gong Day #_____   M T W R F S S   ____/____/20____

Today **I am** Grateful:

■   _____

because_____

■   _____

because_____

■   _____

because_____

Most meaningful **Experience** Journal:

_____
_____
_____
_____
_____
_____
_____
_____
_____
_____
_____
_____
_____
_____
_____
_____
_____
_____
_____

□ *Gong* Day #_____   M T W R F S S   ____ / ____ / 20 ____

Today **I am** Grateful:

- _____

  because_____

- _____

  because_____

- _____

  because_____

Most meaningful **Experience** Journal:

_____
_____
_____
_____
_____
_____
_____
_____
_____
_____
_____
_____
_____
_____
_____
_____
_____
_____
_____

□ Gong Day #_____   M T W R F S S   ____ / ____ / 20 ____

Today **I am** Grateful:

- _____

because_____

- _____

because_____

- _____

because_____

Most meaningful **Experience** Journal:

_____
_____
_____
_____
_____
_____
_____
_____
_____
_____
_____
_____
_____
_____
_____
_____
_____
_____
_____

□ Gong Day #_____   M T W R F S S   ____ / ____ / 20 ____

Today I am Grateful:

- _____

because_____

- _____

because_____

- _____

because_____

Most meaningful Experience Journal:

_____
_____
_____
_____
_____
_____
_____
_____
_____
_____
_____
_____
_____
_____
_____
_____
_____
_____
_____

□ Gong Day #_____ M T W R F S S ____ / ____ / 20 ____

Today I am Grateful:

- _____

because_____

- _____

because_____

- _____

because_____

Most meaningful Experience Journal:

_____
_____
_____
_____
_____
_____
_____
_____
_____
_____
_____
_____
_____
_____
_____
_____
_____
_____

□ *Gong* Day #_____   M T W R F S S   ____ / ____ / 20 ____

Today **I am** Grateful:

- _____

because_____

- _____

because_____

- _____

because_____

Most meaningful **Experience** Journal:

_____
_____
_____
_____
_____
_____
_____
_____
_____
_____
_____
_____
_____
_____
_____
_____
_____
_____
_____

□ Gong Day #_____   M T W R F S S   ____ / ____ / 20 ____

Today **I am** Grateful:

- _____

  because_____

- _____

  because_____

- _____

  because_____

Most meaningful **Experience** Journal:

_____
_____
_____
_____
_____
_____
_____
_____
_____
_____
_____
_____
_____
_____
_____
_____
_____
_____
_____

□ Gong Day #_____   M T W R F S S   ____ / ____ / 20 ____

Today I am Grateful:

- _____

because_____

- _____

because_____

- _____

because_____

Most meaningful Experience Journal:

_____
_____
_____
_____
_____
_____
_____
_____
_____
_____
_____
_____
_____
_____
_____
_____
_____
_____
_____

☐ *Gong* Day #_____   M T W R F S S   ____/____/20____

Today **I am** Grateful:

- _____

because_____

- _____

because_____

- _____

because_____

Most meaningful **Experience** Journal:

_____
_____
_____
_____
_____
_____
_____
_____
_____
_____
_____
_____
_____
_____
_____
_____
_____
_____

□ *Gong* Day #_____   M T W R F S S   ____/ ____/ 20 ____

Today **I am** Grateful:

- _____

  because_____

- _____

  because_____

- _____

  because_____

Most meaningful **Experience** Journal:

_____
_____
_____
_____
_____
_____
_____
_____
_____
_____
_____
_____
_____
_____
_____
_____
_____
_____
_____
_____

□ Gong Day #_____   M T W R F S S   _____ / _____ / 20 _____

Today I am Grateful:

- _____

because_____

- _____

because_____

- _____

because_____

Most meaningful Experience Journal:

_____
_____
_____
_____
_____
_____
_____
_____
_____
_____
_____
_____
_____
_____
_____
_____
_____
_____

□ Gong Day #_____   M T W R F S S   ____ / ____ / 20 ____

Today I am Grateful:

- _____

  because_____

- _____

  because_____

- _____

  because_____

Most meaningful Experience Journal:

_____
_____
_____
_____
_____
_____
_____
_____
_____
_____
_____
_____
_____
_____
_____
_____
_____
_____
_____

☐ Gong Day #_____ M T W R F S S _____ / _____ / 20 _____

Today **I am** Grateful:

- _____

  because_____

- _____

  because_____

- _____

  because_____

Most meaningful **Experience** Journal:

_____
_____
_____
_____
_____
_____
_____
_____
_____
_____
_____
_____
_____
_____
_____
_____
_____
_____

□ Gong Day #_____   M T W R F S S   ____/____/20_____

Today I am Grateful:

- _____

  because_____

- _____

  because_____

- _____

  because_____

Most meaningful Experience Journal:

_____
_____
_____
_____
_____
_____
_____
_____
_____
_____
_____
_____
_____
_____
_____
_____
_____
_____
_____

☐ Gong Day #_____ M T W R F S S _____ / _____ / 20 _____

Today **I am** Grateful:

- _____

because_____

- _____

because_____

- _____

because_____

Most meaningful **Experience** Journal:

_____
_____
_____
_____
_____
_____
_____
_____
_____
_____
_____
_____
_____
_____
_____
_____
_____
_____
_____

□ Gong Day #_____ M T W R F S S ____/____/20____

Today I am Grateful:

- _____

because_____

- _____

because_____

- _____

because_____

Most meaningful Experience Journal:

_____
_____
_____
_____
_____
_____
_____
_____
_____
_____
_____
_____
_____
_____
_____
_____
_____
_____
_____
_____

☐ Gong Day #_____   M T W R F S S   ____ / ____ / 20 ____

Today **I am** Grateful:

- _____

because_____

- _____

because_____

- _____

because_____

Most meaningful **Experience** Journal:

_____
_____
_____
_____
_____
_____
_____
_____
_____
_____
_____
_____
_____
_____
_____
_____
_____
_____

□ *Gong* Day #_____   M T W R F S S   ____ / ____ / 20 ____

Today **I am** Grateful:

■ _____

because_____

■ _____

because_____

■ _____

because_____

Most meaningful **Experience** Journal:

_____
_____
_____
_____
_____
_____
_____
_____
_____
_____
_____
_____
_____
_____
_____
_____
_____
_____
_____
_____

□ Gong Day #_____ M T W R F S S ____/____/20____

Today I am Grateful:

- _____

  because_____

- _____

  because_____

- _____

  because_____

Most meaningful Experience Journal:

_____
_____
_____
_____
_____
_____
_____
_____
_____
_____
_____
_____
_____
_____
_____
_____
_____
_____
_____

□ *Gong* Day #_____ M T W R F S S _____/_____/20_____

Today **I am** Grateful:

- _____

  because_____

- _____

  because_____

- _____

  because_____

Most meaningful **Experience** Journal:

_____
_____
_____
_____
_____
_____
_____
_____
_____
_____
_____
_____
_____
_____
_____
_____
_____
_____
_____

□ Gong Day #_____ M T W R F S S _____/ _____/ 20 _____

Today I am Grateful:

- _____

because_____

- _____

because_____

- _____

because_____

Most meaningful Experience Journal:

_____
_____
_____
_____
_____
_____
_____
_____
_____
_____
_____
_____
_____
_____
_____
_____
_____
_____

□ *Gong* Day #_____   M T W R F S S   ____/____/20____

Today I am Grateful:

■ _____

because_____

■ _____

because_____

■ _____

because_____

Most meaningful Experience Journal:

_____
_____
_____
_____
_____
_____
_____
_____
_____
_____
_____
_____
_____
_____
_____
_____
_____
_____
_____

□ Gong Day #_____   M T W R F S S   ____ / ____ / 20 _____

Today I am Grateful:

- _____

  because_____

- _____

  because_____

- _____

  because_____

Most meaningful Experience Journal:

_____
_____
_____
_____
_____
_____
_____
_____
_____
_____
_____
_____
_____
_____
_____
_____
_____
_____

□ *Gong* Day #_____   M T W R F S S   ____ / ____ / 20 ____

Today **I am** Grateful:

■ _____

because_____

■ _____

because_____

■ _____

because_____

Most meaningful **Experience** Journal:

_____
_____
_____
_____
_____
_____
_____
_____
_____
_____
_____
_____
_____
_____
_____
_____
_____
_____
_____
_____

□ Gong Day #_____   M T W R F S S   ____ / ____ / 20 ____

Today **I am** Grateful:

- _____

  because_____

- _____

  because_____

- _____

  because_____

Most meaningful **Experience** Journal:

_____
_____
_____
_____
_____
_____
_____
_____
_____
_____
_____
_____
_____
_____
_____
_____
_____
_____
_____

□ Gong Day #_____   M T W R F S S   ____ / ____ / 20 ____

Today I am Grateful:

- _____

because_____

- _____

because_____

- _____

because_____

Most meaningful Experience Journal:

_____
_____
_____
_____
_____
_____
_____
_____
_____
_____
_____
_____
_____
_____
_____
_____
_____
_____
_____

☐ *Gong* Day #_____ M T W R F S S ____ / ____ / 20 ____

Today **I am** Grateful:

- _____

  because_____

- _____

  because_____

- _____

  because_____

Most meaningful **Experience** Journal:

_____
_____
_____
_____
_____
_____
_____
_____
_____
_____
_____
_____
_____
_____
_____
_____
_____
_____
_____
_____

□ Gong Day #_____ M T W R F S S _____ / _____ / 20 _____

Today **I am** Grateful:

- _____

  because_____

- _____

  because_____

- _____

  because_____

Most meaningful **Experience** Journal:

_____
_____
_____
_____
_____
_____
_____
_____
_____
_____
_____
_____
_____
_____
_____
_____
_____
_____
_____

□ Gong Day #_____   M T W R F S S   ____ / ____ / 20 ____

Today I am Grateful:

- _____

  because_____

- _____

  because_____

- _____

  because_____

Most meaningful Experience Journal:

_____
_____
_____
_____
_____
_____
_____
_____
_____
_____
_____
_____
_____
_____
_____
_____
_____
_____

☐ Gong Day #_____ M T W R F S S _____ / _____ / 20 _____

Today I am Grateful:

- _____

  because_____

- _____

  because_____

- _____

  because_____

Most meaningful Experience Journal:

_____
_____
_____
_____
_____
_____
_____
_____
_____
_____
_____
_____
_____
_____
_____
_____
_____
_____
_____

☐ Gong Day #_____ M T W R F S S ____/____/20____

Today **I am** Grateful:

- _____

  because_____

- _____

  because_____

- _____

  because_____

Most meaningful **Experience** Journal:

_____

_____

_____

_____

_____

_____

_____

_____

_____

_____

_____

_____

_____

_____

_____

_____

_____

□ *Gong* Day #_____ M T W R F S S ____/ ____/ 20 _____

Today **I am** Grateful:

■ _____

because_____

■ _____

because_____

■ _____

because_____

Most meaningful **Experience** Journal:

_____
_____
_____
_____
_____
_____
_____
_____
_____
_____
_____
_____
_____
_____
_____
_____
_____
_____
_____

□ *Gong* Day #_____   M T W R F S S   _____ / _____ / 20 _____

Today **I am** Grateful:

- _____

because_____

- _____

because_____

- _____

because_____

Most meaningful **Experience** Journal:

_____
_____
_____
_____
_____
_____
_____
_____
_____
_____
_____
_____
_____
_____
_____
_____
_____
_____

□ Gong Day #_____   M T W R F S S   ____ / ____ / 20 ____

Today I am Grateful:

- _____

  because_____

- _____

  because_____

- _____

  because_____

Most meaningful Experience Journal:

_____
_____
_____
_____
_____
_____
_____
_____
_____
_____
_____
_____
_____
_____
_____
_____
_____
_____

□ Gong Day #_____   M T W R F S S   ____ / ____ / 20 _____

Today **I am** Grateful:

- _____

because_____

- _____

because_____

- _____

because_____

Most meaningful **Experience** Journal:

_____
_____
_____
_____
_____
_____
_____
_____
_____
_____
_____
_____
_____
_____
_____
_____
_____
_____

☐ Gong Day #_____ M T W R F S S _____/_____/20_____

Today I am Grateful:

- _____

  because_____

- _____

  because_____

- _____

  because_____

Most meaningful Experience Journal:

_____
_____
_____
_____
_____
_____
_____
_____
_____
_____
_____
_____
_____
_____
_____
_____
_____
_____
_____

□ Gong Day #_____   M T W R F S S   ____ / ____ / 20 ____

Today I am Grateful:

- _____

  because_____

- _____

  because_____

- _____

  because_____

Most meaningful Experience Journal:

_____
_____
_____
_____
_____
_____
_____
_____
_____
_____
_____
_____
_____
_____
_____
_____
_____
_____

□ Gong Day #_____   M T W R F S S   ____ / ____ / 20 ____

Today I am Grateful:

- _____

  because_____

- _____

  because_____

- _____

  because_____

Most meaningful Experience Journal:

_____

_____

_____

_____

_____

_____

_____

_____

_____

_____

_____

_____

_____

_____

_____

_____

_____

_____

_____

□ Gong Day #_____   M T W R F S S ____ / ____ / 20 ____

Today I am Grateful:

- _____

because_____

- _____

because_____

- _____

because_____

Most meaningful Experience Journal:

_____
_____
_____
_____
_____
_____
_____
_____
_____
_____
_____
_____
_____
_____
_____
_____
_____
_____

□ Gong Day #_____   M T W R F S S   ____ / ____ / 20 ____

Today I am Grateful:

- _____

because_____

- _____

because_____

- _____

because_____

Most meaningful Experience Journal:

_____
_____
_____
_____
_____
_____
_____
_____
_____
_____
_____
_____
_____
_____
_____
_____
_____
_____
_____

□ Gong Day #_____   M T W R F S S   ____/ ____/ 20 ____

Today I am Grateful:

- _____

  because_____

- _____

  because_____

- _____

  because_____

Most meaningful Experience Journal:

_____
_____
_____
_____
_____
_____
_____
_____
_____
_____
_____
_____
_____
_____
_____
_____
_____
_____

□ *Gong* Day #_____   M T W R F S S   ____/____/20____

Today **I am** Grateful:

- _____

  because_____

- _____

  because_____

- _____

  because_____

Most meaningful **Experience** Journal:

_____
_____
_____
_____
_____
_____
_____
_____
_____
_____
_____
_____
_____
_____
_____
_____
_____
_____
_____

☐ Gong Day #_____   M T W R F S S   _____ / _____ / 20 _____

Today I am Grateful:

- _____

because_____

- _____

because_____

- _____

because_____

Most meaningful Experience Journal:

_____
_____
_____
_____
_____
_____
_____
_____
_____
_____
_____
_____
_____
_____
_____
_____
_____
_____
_____

□ Gong Day #_____ M T W R F S S _____ / _____ / 20 _____

Today I am Grateful:

- _____

because_____

- _____

because_____

- _____

because_____

Most meaningful Experience Journal:

_____

_____

_____

_____

_____

_____

_____

_____

_____

_____

_____

_____

_____

_____

_____

_____

_____

_____

□ Gong Day #_____   M T W R F S S   _____ / _____ / 20 _____

Today **I am** Grateful:

- _____

because_____

- _____

because_____

- _____

because_____

Most meaningful **Experience** Journal:

_____

_____

_____

_____

_____

_____

_____

_____

_____

_____

_____

_____

_____

_____

_____

_____

_____

_____

_____

□ Gong Day #_____ M T W R F S S ____/____/20____

Today I am Grateful:

- _____

  because_____

- _____

  because_____

- _____

  because_____

Most meaningful Experience Journal:

_____
_____
_____
_____
_____
_____
_____
_____
_____
_____
_____
_____
_____
_____
_____
_____
_____
_____
_____
_____

□ Gong Day #_____   M T W R F S S   ___ / ___ / 20 ___

Today I am Grateful:

- _____

  because_____

- _____

  because_____

- _____

  because_____

Most meaningful Experience Journal:

_____
_____
_____
_____
_____
_____
_____
_____
_____
_____
_____
_____
_____
_____
_____
_____
_____
_____
_____

□ Gong Day #_____ M T W R F S S ____/____/20____

Today I am Grateful:

- _____

  because_____

- _____

  because_____

- _____

  because_____

Most meaningful Experience Journal:

_____
_____
_____
_____
_____
_____
_____
_____
_____
_____
_____
_____
_____
_____
_____
_____
_____
_____
_____

☐ Gong Day #_____   M T W R F S S   ____ / ____ / 20 ____

Today **I am** Grateful:

- _____

  because_____

- _____

  because_____

- _____

  because_____

Most meaningful **Experience** Journal:

_____
_____
_____
_____
_____
_____
_____
_____
_____
_____
_____
_____
_____
_____
_____
_____
_____
_____

□ Gong Day #_____   M T W R F S S   ____ / ____ / 20 ____

Today I am Grateful:

- _____

because_____

- _____

because_____

- _____

because_____

Most meaningful Experience Journal:

_____
_____
_____
_____
_____
_____
_____
_____
_____
_____
_____
_____
_____
_____
_____
_____
_____
_____

□ Gong Day #_____   M T W R F S S   ____ / ____ / 20 ____

Today **I am** Grateful:

- _____

  because_____

- _____

  because_____

- _____

  because_____

Most meaningful **Experience** Journal:

_____
_____
_____
_____
_____
_____
_____
_____
_____
_____
_____
_____
_____
_____
_____
_____
_____
_____
_____
_____
_____

□ Gong Day #_____   M T W R F S S   ____ / ____ / 20 ____

Today I am Grateful:

- _____

  because_____

- _____

  because_____

- _____

  because_____

Most meaningful Experience Journal:

_____
_____
_____
_____
_____
_____
_____
_____
_____
_____
_____
_____
_____
_____
_____
_____
_____
_____
_____

□ *Gong* Day #_____   M T W R F S S   _____ / _____ / 20 _____

Today **I am** Grateful:

- _____

  because_____

- _____

  because_____

- _____

  because_____

Most meaningful **Experience** Journal:

_____
_____
_____
_____
_____
_____
_____
_____
_____
_____
_____
_____
_____
_____
_____
_____
_____
_____
_____
_____

□ Gong Day #_____ M T W R F S S _____ / _____ / 20 _____

Today I am Grateful:

- _____

  because_____

- _____

  because_____

- _____

  because_____

Most meaningful Experience Journal:

_____
_____
_____
_____
_____
_____
_____
_____
_____
_____
_____
_____
_____
_____
_____
_____
_____
_____
_____

☐ Gong Day #_____   M T W R F S S   ____ / ____ / 20 ____

Today I am Grateful:

- _____

because_____

- _____

because_____

- _____

because_____

Most meaningful Experience Journal:

_____
_____
_____
_____
_____
_____
_____
_____
_____
_____
_____
_____
_____
_____
_____
_____
_____
_____
_____
_____

□ *Gong* Day #_____ M T W R F S S ____/____/ 20 ____

Today **I am** Grateful:

- _____

because_____

- _____

because_____

- _____

because_____

Most meaningful **Experience** Journal:

_____
_____
_____
_____
_____
_____
_____
_____
_____
_____
_____
_____
_____
_____
_____
_____
_____
_____

☐ Gong Day #_____ M T W R F S S ____/____/20____

Today I am Grateful:

- _____

  because_____

- _____

  because_____

- _____

  because_____

Most meaningful Experience Journal:

_____
_____
_____
_____
_____
_____
_____
_____
_____
_____
_____
_____
_____
_____
_____
_____
_____
_____

□ *Gong* Day #_____   M T W R F S S   _____ / _____ / 20 _____

Today I *am* Grateful:

- _____

because_____

- _____

because_____

- _____

because_____

Most meaningful **Experience** Journal:

_____
_____
_____
_____
_____
_____
_____
_____
_____
_____
_____
_____
_____
_____
_____
_____
_____
_____
_____

□ Gong Day #_____   M T W R F S S   ____ / ____ / 20 ____

Today **I am** Grateful:

- _____

because_____

- _____

because_____

- _____

because_____

Most meaningful **Experience** Journal:

_____
_____
_____
_____
_____
_____
_____
_____
_____
_____
_____
_____
_____
_____
_____
_____
_____
_____
_____

□ Gong Day #_____ M T W R F S S ___ / ___ / 20 ___

Today I am Grateful:

- _____

because_____

- _____

because_____

- _____

because_____

Most meaningful Experience Journal:

_____
_____
_____
_____
_____
_____
_____
_____
_____
_____
_____
_____
_____
_____
_____
_____
_____
_____
_____

☐ Gong Day #_____   M T W R F S S   ____ / ____ / 20 ____

Today **I am** Grateful:

- _____

  because_____

- _____

  because_____

- _____

  because_____

Most meaningful **Experience** Journal:

_____
_____
_____
_____
_____
_____
_____
_____
_____
_____
_____
_____
_____
_____
_____
_____
_____
_____

☐ Gong Day #_____ M T W R F S S _____/_____/20_____

Today **I am** Grateful:

- _____

  because_____

- _____

  because_____

- _____

  because_____

Most meaningful **Experience** Journal:

_____

_____

_____

_____

_____

_____

_____

_____

_____

_____

_____

_____

_____

_____

_____

_____

_____

_____

_____

☐ Gong Day #_____   M T W R F S S   ____ / ____ / 20 ____

Today I am Grateful:

- _____

because_____

- _____

because_____

- _____

because_____

Most meaningful Experience Journal:

_____
_____
_____
_____
_____
_____
_____
_____
_____
_____
_____
_____
_____
_____
_____
_____
_____
_____

□ *Gong* Day #_____   M T W R F S S   ____/____/20____

Today **I am** Grateful:

- _____

because_____

- _____

because_____

- _____

because_____

Most meaningful **Experience** Journal:

_____
_____
_____
_____
_____
_____
_____
_____
_____
_____
_____
_____
_____
_____
_____
_____
_____
_____
_____

□ Gong Day #_____   M T W R F S S   _____ / _____ / 20 _____

Today **I am** Grateful:

- _____

  because_____

- _____

  because_____

- _____

  because_____

Most meaningful **Experience** Journal:

_____
_____
_____
_____
_____
_____
_____
_____
_____
_____
_____
_____
_____
_____
_____
_____
_____
_____

□ Gong Day #_____   M T W R F S S   ____/ ____/ 20 _____

Today I am Grateful:

- _____

because_____

- _____

because_____

- _____

because_____

Most meaningful Experience Journal:

_____
_____
_____
_____
_____
_____
_____
_____
_____
_____
_____
_____
_____
_____
_____
_____
_____
_____
_____
_____

☐ Gong Day #_____   M T W R F S S   _____ / _____ / 20 _____

Today I am Grateful:

- _____

  because_____

- _____

  because_____

- _____

  because_____

Most meaningful Experience Journal:

_____
_____
_____
_____
_____
_____
_____
_____
_____
_____
_____
_____
_____
_____
_____
_____
_____
_____
_____

☐ *Gong* Day #_____   M T W R F S S   ____ / ____ / 20 ____

Today **I am** Grateful:

■ _____

because_____

■ _____

because_____

■ _____

because_____

Most meaningful **Experience** Journal:

☐ *Gong* Day #_____ M T W R F S S ____ / ____ / 20 ____

Today **I am** Grateful:

■ _____

because_____

■ _____

because_____

■ _____

because_____

Most meaningful **Experience** Journal:

_____
_____
_____
_____
_____
_____
_____
_____
_____
_____
_____
_____
_____
_____
_____
_____
_____
_____
_____
_____

□ Gong Day #_____   M T W R F S S   ____ / ____ / 20 ____

Today I am Grateful:

■ _____

because_____

■ _____

because_____

■ _____

because_____

Most meaningful Experience Journal:

_____
_____
_____
_____
_____
_____
_____
_____
_____
_____
_____
_____
_____
_____
_____
_____
_____
_____
_____

□ Gong Day #_____   M T W R F S S   _____ / _____ / 20 _____

Today **I am** Grateful:

- _____

because_____

- _____

because_____

- _____

because_____

Most meaningful **Experience** Journal:

_____
_____
_____
_____
_____
_____
_____
_____
_____
_____
_____
_____
_____
_____
_____
_____
_____
_____
_____

☐ *Gong* Day #_____   M   T   W   R   F   S   S   ____ / ____ / 20 ____

Today **I am** Grateful:

- _____

  because_____

- _____

  because_____

- _____

  because_____

Most meaningful **Experience** Journal:

_____
_____
_____
_____
_____
_____
_____
_____
_____
_____
_____
_____
_____
_____
_____
_____
_____
_____
_____
_____

☐ Gong Day #_____ M T W R F S S _____ / _____ / 20 _____

Today **I am** Grateful:

- _____

because_____

- _____

because_____

- _____

because_____

Most meaningful **Experience** Journal:

_____
_____
_____
_____
_____
_____
_____
_____
_____
_____
_____
_____
_____
_____
_____
_____
_____
_____

□ *Gong* Day #_____ M T W R F S S _____ / _____ / 20 _____

Today **I am** Grateful:

- _____

  because_____

- _____

  because_____

- _____

  because_____

Most meaningful **Experience** Journal:

_____
_____
_____
_____
_____
_____
_____
_____
_____
_____
_____
_____
_____
_____
_____
_____
_____
_____

☐ Gong Day #_____   M T W R F S S   ____ / ____ / 20 ____

Today I am Grateful:

- _____

  because_____

- _____

  because_____

- _____

  because_____

Most meaningful Experience Journal:

_____
_____
_____
_____
_____
_____
_____
_____
_____
_____
_____
_____
_____
_____
_____
_____
_____
_____

□ **Gong** Day #_____ M T W R F S S _____ / _____ / 20 _____

Today **I am** Grateful:

■ _____

because_____

■ _____

because_____

■ _____

because_____

Most meaningful **Experience** Journal:

_____
_____
_____
_____
_____
_____
_____
_____
_____
_____
_____
_____
_____
_____
_____
_____
_____
_____
_____

□ Gong Day #_____ M T W R F S S ____/____/20____

Today I am Grateful:

- _____

  because_____

- _____

  because_____

- _____

  because_____

Most meaningful Experience Journal:

_____
_____
_____
_____
_____
_____
_____
_____
_____
_____
_____
_____
_____
_____
_____
_____
_____
_____
_____
_____

□ Gong Day #_____ M T W R F S S _____/_____/20_____

Today I am Grateful:

- _____

  because_____

- _____

  because_____

- _____

  because_____

Most meaningful Experience Journal:

_____
_____
_____
_____
_____
_____
_____
_____
_____
_____
_____
_____
_____
_____
_____
_____
_____
_____
_____

□ Gong Day #_____   M T W R F S S   ____ / ____ / 20 ____

Today **I am** Grateful:

- _____

  because_____

- _____

  because_____

- _____

  because_____

Most meaningful **Experience** Journal:

_____
_____
_____
_____
_____
_____
_____
_____
_____
_____
_____
_____
_____
_____
_____
_____
_____
_____

□ Gong Day #_____ M T W R F S S ____/____/ 20____

Today I am Grateful:

- _____

  because_____

- _____

  because_____

- _____

  because_____

Most meaningful Experience Journal:

_____
_____
_____
_____
_____
_____
_____
_____
_____
_____
_____
_____
_____
_____
_____
_____
_____
_____
_____

□ Gong Day #_____   M T W R F S S   _____ / _____ / 20 _____

Today I am Grateful:

- _____

because_____

- _____

because_____

- _____

because_____

Most meaningful Experience Journal:

_____
_____
_____
_____
_____
_____
_____
_____
_____
_____
_____
_____
_____
_____
_____
_____
_____
_____
_____
_____

☐ *Gong* Day #_____   M T W R F S S   ____ / ____ / 20 _____

Today **I am** Grateful:

■ _____

because_____

■ _____

because_____

■ _____

because_____

Most meaningful **Experience** Journal:

_____
_____
_____
_____
_____
_____
_____
_____
_____
_____
_____
_____
_____
_____
_____
_____
_____
_____
_____

□ Gong Day #_____   M T W R F S S   ____/ ____/ 20 ____

Today I am Grateful:

- _____

because_____

- _____

because_____

- _____

because_____

Most meaningful Experience Journal:

_____
_____
_____
_____
_____
_____
_____
_____
_____
_____
_____
_____
_____
_____
_____
_____
_____
_____

☐ *Gong* Day #_____ M T W R F S S ___ / ___ / 20 ____

Today **I am** Grateful:

- _____

  because_____

- _____

  because_____

- _____

  because_____

Most meaningful **Experience** Journal:

□ Gong Day #_____ M T W R F S S _____ / _____ / 20 _____

Today **I am** Grateful:

- _____

because_____

- _____

because_____

- _____

because_____

Most meaningful **Experience** Journal:

_____
_____
_____
_____
_____
_____
_____
_____
_____
_____
_____
_____
_____
_____
_____
_____
_____
_____
_____

☐ *Gong* Day #_____ M T W R F S S _____ / _____ / 20 _____

Today I **am** Grateful:

- _____

  because_____

- _____

  because_____

- _____

  because_____

Most meaningful **Experience** Journal:

_____
_____
_____
_____
_____
_____
_____
_____
_____
_____
_____
_____
_____
_____
_____
_____
_____
_____
_____

☐ Gong Day #_____ M T W R F S S ____/ ____/ 20 ____

Today I am Grateful:

- _____

because_____

- _____

because_____

- _____

because_____

Most meaningful Experience Journal:

_____

_____

_____

_____

_____

_____

_____

_____

_____

_____

_____

_____

_____

_____

_____

_____

_____

□ Gong Day #_____   M T W R F S S   ____ / ____ / 20 ____

Today I am Grateful:

■ _____

because_____

■ _____

because_____

■ _____

because_____

Most meaningful Experience Journal:

_____

_____

_____

_____

_____

_____

_____

_____

_____

_____

_____

_____

_____

_____

_____

_____

_____

_____

_____

NOTES:

NOTES:

NOTES:

CONGRATULATIONS!

When you complete your gong, it's time to celebrate!

You may choose to do one gong every year, or maybe three. You may decide to do two at once some years. Whatever you decide, your work during the gong will serve you and the people in your life for years to come.

Stay curious and open to new possibilities. When you are ready, begin again. Invite a friend to join you. Let's make our world happier and healthier one gong at a time.

ABOUT THE AUTHOR

Melissa Jones, DDS is the founder of Carson City Orthodontics where she leads a team whose mission is to help others Smile... and Feel Good! She loves to explore topics of health and happiness, and dedicates many hours each week to learning from wellness experts via podcasts, books, and courses. Her goal is to share the most helpful happiness hacks that she discovers with teams and teens who otherwise wouldn't have time to learn about them. She believes that inspiring coworkers and youth will generate health and happiness for entire communities and the world at large. To learn more or share additional resources, visit carsoncityortho.com/community-outreach

Made in the
USA
Middletown, DE